Doors

Doors

SELECTED BY BOB WILCOX

FOREWORD BY JEROME MARKSON

FIREFLY BOOKS

A FIREFLY BOOK

Published by Firefly Books Ltd. 2009
Copyright © 2009 Firefly Books Ltd.
Foreword copyright © 2009 Jerome Markson
Introduction copyright © 2009 Bob Wilcox
Images copyright as listed in Credits beginning on page 263
All rights reserved.

First printing

Publisher Cataloging-in-Publication Data (U.S.)
Wilcox, Bob.
    Doors/ Bob Wilcox.
[272] p. : col. photos. ; cm.
Includes index.
Summary: Photographs of doors from around the world.
ISBN-13: 978-1-55407-550-8
ISBN-10: 1-55407-550-5
1. Doorways. 2. Doors. I. Title.
721.822   dc22   NA3010.W553 2009

Library and Archives Canada Cataloguing in Publication
Wilcox, Bob, 1941-
    Doors / selected by Bob Wilcox ;
    foreword by Jerome Markson.
Includes index.
ISBN-13: 978-1-55407-550-8
ISBN-10: 1-55407-550-5
    1. Doors—Pictorial works.   I. Title.
NA3010.W45 2009   721'.8220222   C2009-901503-X

Published in the United States by
Firefly Books (U.S.) Inc.
P.O. Box 1338, Ellicott Station
Buffalo, New York 14205

Published in Canada by
Firefly Books Ltd.
66 Leek Crescent
Richmond Hill, Ontario L4B 1H1

The publisher gratefully acknowledges the financial support for our publishing program by the Government of Canada through the Book Publishing Industry Development Program.

Cover and interior design by Bob Wilcox
Layout by Tinge Design Studio
Printed in China

FOREWORD

As an architect, immersing myself in the richness revealed in the pages of this book, I wonder why there is such a paucity of imagination and effort given to the design of doors and entranceways today. Most architecturally designed entrances are now minimalist in character – just a plain slab of stone or metal, or a clear sheet of safety glass. The only readily available alternative seems to be a mass-produced product of machine-punched panels, utterly devoid of originality or meaning.

Why are we so inhibited when our ancestors let their imagination produce functional doors of great beauty and meaning? Is it the cost of building, or have we been brainwashed into believing that everything must be functionally designed with no other purpose than to provide an entrance and exit? Whatever the reason, *Doors* gives us a chance to step back, renew our focus and enliven our work further by absorbing the varied lessons of world culture written in these doors.

These photographs reflect the attitudes and ideas of beauty through many periods, cultures and religions from ancient to modern times. The structure of the doors themselves, with their exposed bolts, rivets and panels in patterns, make a statement about the love, passion and care with which they were created to all who pass by. On so many of these old doors, studs are found everywhere; and there are ancient and tattered locks, worn keyholes and well-used knockers that speak of generations of use. Even functional items like hinges, locks, doorbells and knobs are frequently beautiful as well as functional. Some carved wood doors are works of art, with signage – providing the street name and number – that is also often as beautiful as it is informative. The ancient doorways and arches that remain today are of stone since most of the wood has long rotted away or been removed.

These photographs provide a wealth of detail to linger over and enjoy. In many cultures where life is lived in small villages and towns, the streets are lined with whitewashed blank walls that are broken only by the openings for doors and arches. Looking through openings provides a view into the mystery of brilliant, sunlit court-yards beyond, many with vibrant shades that add further magic to the riot of color in the plants and land and ocean around them.

But the doors in this book are not all about beauty. Doors and entranceways have diverse meanings. They provide security from enemies and from danger. And they make a powerful statement about the state, church or association that created them. On private homes, doors suggest the homeowner's social position relative to others in the community and confer instant status.

On many doors, decoration intensifies intention. Sculptures telling the Christian story surmount the entrances to cathedrals. Other examples include the shape, size and fit of the dry stone of the Incas that seem to speak of a world created on a scale too grand for mortal man. In Egypt, gigantic statues of seated kings flank the opening into the ruler's tomb. The intricate maze of figures and heads on Asian monuments reveals a world of complex richness in contrast to the plain but intensely colored doors and surroundings of simple Aegean domestic architecture.

The doors in this book invite us to look carefully to find hidden mysteries that lie beyond. Throughout the history of architecture, entrances have been one of the most expressive parts of buildings. Here are narrow doors, wide doors, exotic and peculiarly shaped doors, together reflecting the myriad ways in which architects and builders have sought to render their buildings as expressions of the cultures in which these structures were created.

Jerome Markson

INTRODUCTION

At the most basic level, doors are simply a way to enter and leave a building. Beyond those purely functional purposes, however, doors have a fascinating and complicated story to tell. Photographers are infatuated with doors. Writers have used doors as metaphors. Architects, artists and craftspeople have designed and created them in wide variety of shapes and forms. Some are mundane, everyday objects suitable for closets, while others are extravagant statements about beauty, power and religion.

Given all the variety available, the search for images of doors to include in this book has been a combination of travelog, history lesson and design symposium. The period I wanted to cover was from the earliest existing examples to the most modern architectural extravaganzas. I also wanted to cover all countries, all styles and all materials. Being this inclusive is a great idea, but it was complicated to implement. When I researched the earliest dwellings still in existence (houses in Ukraine made of mammoth bones 15,000 years ago), I found no information about their doors. There were no photographs and no descriptions. I looked at images of neolithic villages in Scotland, the Temple of Ramses II at Abu Simbel in Egypt, built in 1265 BC, and mud structures built in caves in Mali by bands of pygmies in the 14th century. None of the doors to these structures has survived. Wooden doors or skins, of course, will not last thousands of years. Doors of some important ancient buildings were made of stone and rotated on pivots, and later doors were made of bronze or of wood encased in bronze. Stone doors and bronze encasement can now be seen mostly in museums. What I found were images of buildings with openings where doors could have been, but do not exist at this time. My solution for the earliest buildings I wanted to include was just to show the openings where doors could have been and leave the rest to your imagination.

Ancient doorways without doors have a parallel in contemporary architecture. Modern doors can be elusive. While looking for images of modern doors I found that, in a photograph, glass doors can be mistaken for windows, or be invisible entirely. The very common modern glass door functions as a physical but not a visual barrier. You are literally outside looking in.

Some doors are deliberately designed to remain undetected, looking like a section of the wall except for a tell-tale door-knob. In grand old houses, the doors for the use of servants were intended to be unobtrusive so the servants could come and go to perform their duties while being as invisible as possible. Occasionally, doors were disguised as bookshelves, wall hangings or wood paneling to provide a secret opening to a hidden space.

Doors can be made of many different materials, with a variety of construction techniques, but the door is more than just the panel that covers an opening in a building. In order to function, the door must have accessories. The door needs to hinge or pivot. It must stay closed and lock when necessary. Sometimes it has a window, peep-hole or mail-slot, and is identified with numbers and names. In order for the door to function, you have to interact physically with the door by pushing, pulling or turning something – perhaps a handle, door-knob or lever, combined with a key. Sometimes you have to say your name, or make a sound with a bell, buzzer or knocker. The door could be massive and difficult to move, or flimsy and easily opened. You may be able to see through glass to the inside of the building, or the interior could be a mystery until the door is opened. The sum of these things – structural elements, accessories, and the way you interact when using it – creates the character of the door.

I have not tried to show every possible kind of door. Some doors that perform their required function are not very interesting to look at. Most images I saw of cat and dog doors were boring, as were doors to kitchen cupboards, closets and bath-room cubicles. However, I did find a wonderful stone structure for goats. It has doors for the animals accessible from an exterior spiraling ramp, leading into a tall, thin, multi-storied tower.

The door and its context – the forms, colors and materials surrounding the opening – provide visual signals indicating not only that it is a point of entry but also some aspects of the wealth and status of the occupants. Doors can be intimidating, welcoming, humorous, pompous and just about anything else that can be imagined and built. Frequently the intention of the embellishments that surround a door is difficult to determine for someone from a different culture or a different time. What could have been the reason for the giant, naked, stone torsos flanking a door and holding up a balcony of the Fünf Höfe in Munich? What was the designer thinking of when he created a doorway in Rome resembling a huge head, with a wooden mouth for the door? What goes through the mind of the people who enter these doors? Should they be fearful? Is the door a statement of power? Are the naked giants there to indicate the sensuality to be found within? Should we enjoy them as art or as humor? Whatever you make of them, what's wonderful about these doors is that they are in public places for everyone to enjoy.

Some doors subtly address serious aspects of life. In Japanese tea houses, the tea ceremony was considered the embodiment of aspects of Zen Buddhism. The doors of Japanese tea houses were short so the person entering had to bow slightly in order to get through. Bowing shows courtesy and humility. The doors at the main entrance of medieval cathedrals were huge beyond anything required on a human scale, made to a size considered suitable for a structure built to worship God. Depending on your point of view, these are doors that create feelings of respect, awe, intimidation or thoughts about the nature of your place in the world. Set into these large doors is a small door scaled to human use.

Some of the doors in the photographs I selected are not in perfect condition. They have not been continuously maintained in order to always look new. Doors can be beautiful when they are worn and show their age, when materials have developed the natural patina created by continued use and weather over a very long time. Many travelers visit other countries to see exactly that – worn stone and wood, bleached paint, rust and oxidation that with time, change familiar objects into unique works of art.

Sometimes the structure of the door is an opportunity to use textures, colors or building materials that are different from the rest of the building. In some photographs, the door is the only extravagant element on a building that is otherwise much more restrained. On the Greek islands, the tradition is to paint the walls and walkways white and most of the doors turquoise-blue, which unifies the entire village and makes the doors stand out.

I found an interesting door that was designed to deal with environmental issues. On the coast of Wales, the doors and a metal chimney are the only visible elements of an underground house, designed in a way that reduces the impact of human habitation on a sensitive sea cliff site. The door is set into a grassy hill that forms the wall and roof of the house. The feeling this door gives is similar to that of troglodyte doors set into openings of caves carved into rock walls – a manmade doorway into the earth itself.

My front door is not in this book. I like the color, and the design is appropriate for the building I live in, but it is an ordinary example of 1950s architecture and design. The door doesn't have paper screens or medieval hardware. It is not old or mysterious and has not, to my knowledge, been photographed by passersby. It's unlikely I will change it, despite having seen thousands of more interesting doors in preparing this book. My door is appropriate to its surroundings and purpose. But on these pages I have had a wonderful opportunity to visit other buildings, other countries and other times to see what they made of this fascinating, necessary and sometimes mysterious object. I hope you enjoy the journey as much as I have enjoyed being your guide.

Bob Wilcox

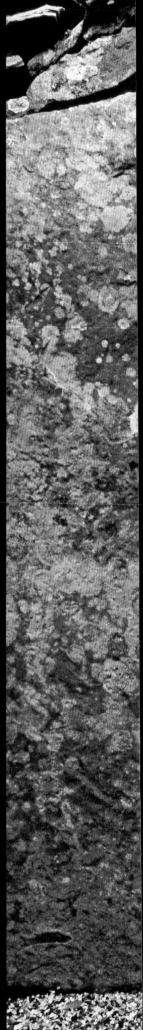

22

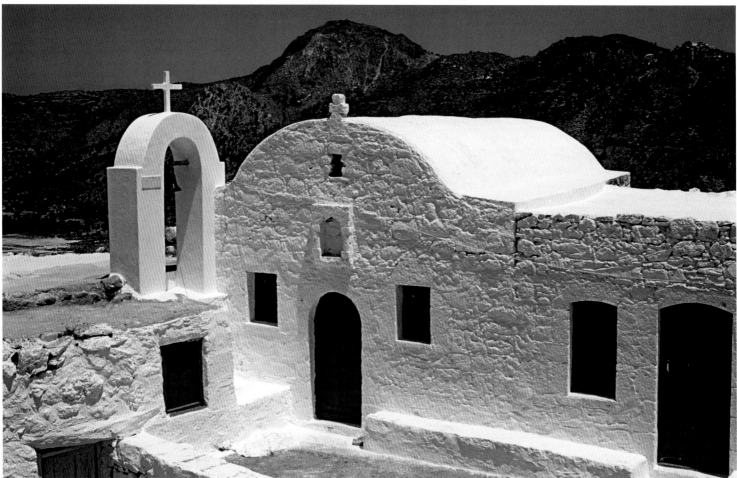

36

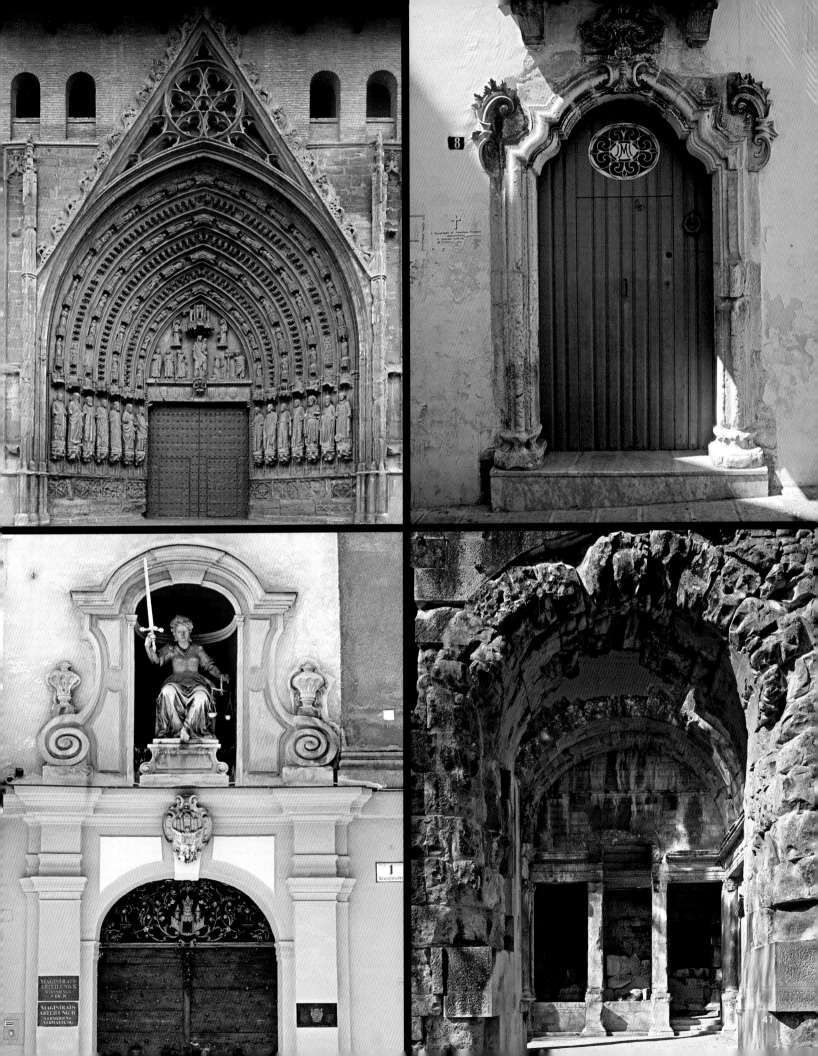

42

Faulhaber-Str.

44

48

48

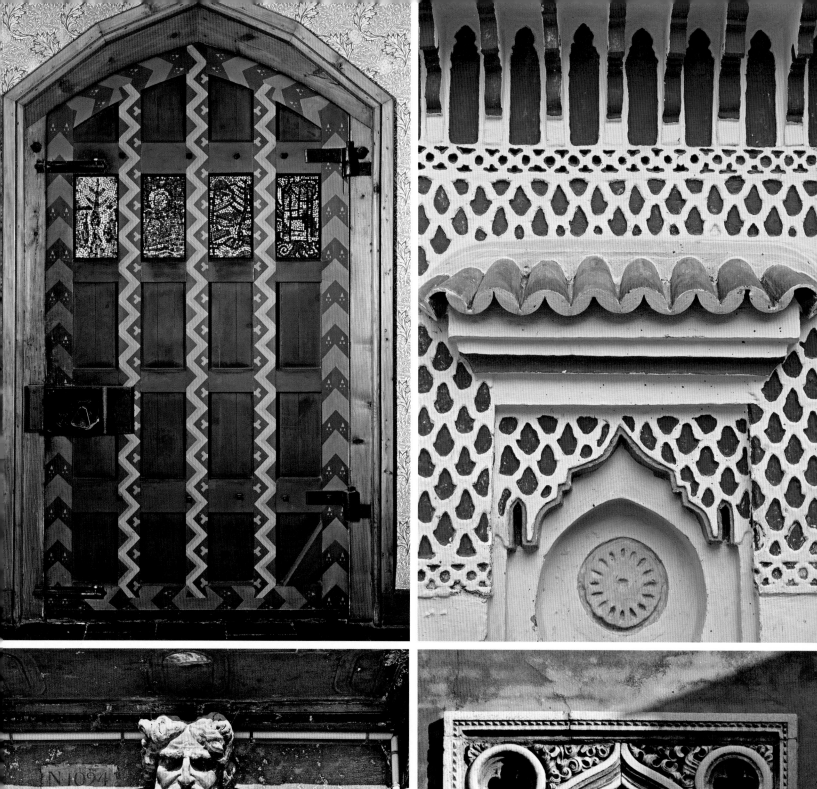

58

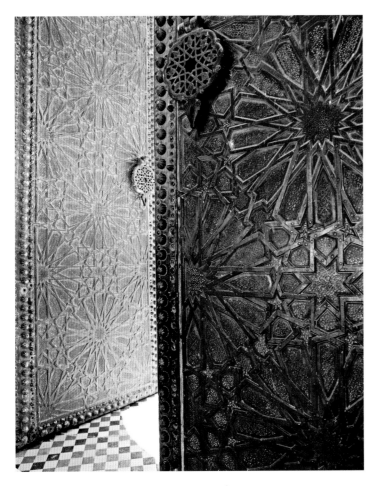

91

OROLOGER A

HORARIO
• DE •
8 AM. A 1 PM.
- Y -
4:30 A 7:30 PM.
BOT. DE 7·50 ML.
PRECIO $20·00

• •
RON
• •

97

108

門前綠水環遶帶

戶外青山列錦屏

ESTUDI METRO

316

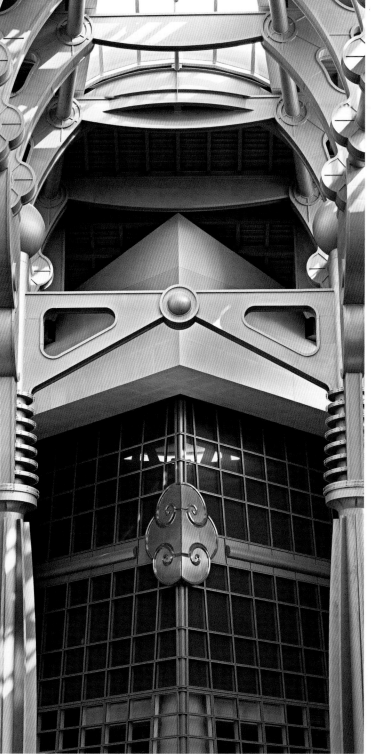

183

FIRST LORD OF THE TREASURY

198

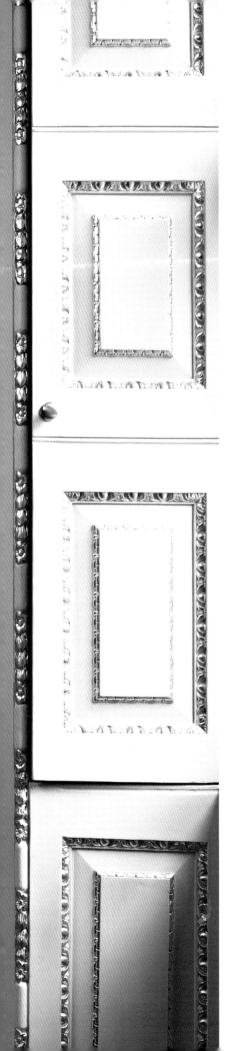

201

204

225

CACTACEAE
Mammelaria sp.
Mexico

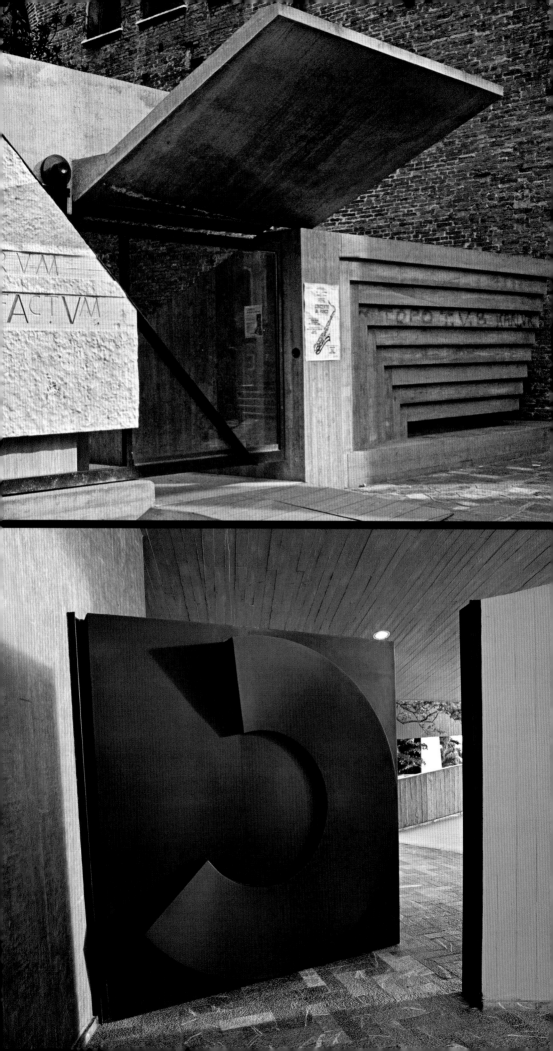

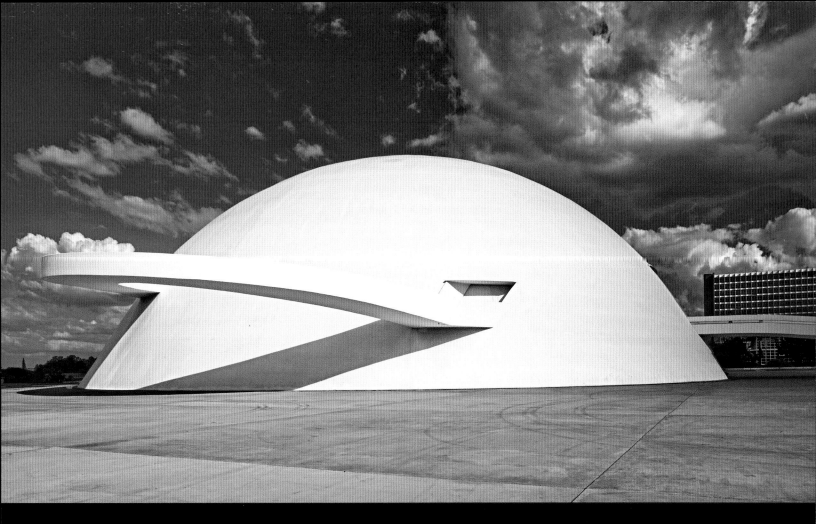

THE SAVILL BUILDING

261

PHOTO CREDITS

12 Trapezoidal Inca doorway with lintel, Sacsahuaman, Peru. Nick Saunders/WERNER FORMAN/arcaid.co.uk

13 Orkney Islands, Scotland. Werner Forman/WERNER FORMAN/arcaid.co.uk

14 Pyramid of Cheops. Cairo Egypt. Werner Forman/WERNER FORMAN/arcaid.co.uk.

15 Ramses II Temple, Abu Simbel, Egypt. Marcel Malherbe/arcaid.co.uk.

16 TOP Bandiagara cliffs. Sanga, Mali. Werner Forman/WERNER FORMAN/arcaid.co.uk.

16 BOTTOM Mud relief and elaborate paintings on the wall of a Dogon shrine. Werner Forman/WERNER FORMAN/arcaid.co.uk.

17 TOP Pompeii, Italy. Werner Forman/WERNER FORMAN/arcaid.co.uk.

17 BOTTOM LEFT Riyadh, Saudi Arabia. Robert O'Dea/arcaid.co.uk.

18 TOP Hal Saflieni Hypogeum. Paola, Malta. Werner Forman/WERNER FORMAN/arcaid.co.uk.

18 BOTTOM Kom-El-Shuqafa tomb, Alexandria, Egypt. Werner Forman/WERNER FORMAN/arcaid.co.uk

19 Kano, Nigeria. Werner Forman/WERNER FORMAN/arcaid.co.uk.

20 TOP Angkor Wat West Gateway. Angkor Wat, Cambodia. Natalie Tepper/arcaid.co.uk.

20 BOTTOM Ta Prohm Temple in the jungle. Siem Reap, Cambodia. Rainer Kiedrowski/Bildarchiv-Monheim/arcaid.co.uk.

21 Angkor Wat West Gateway. Angkor Wat, Cambodia. Natalie Tepper/arcaid.co.uk.

22 TOP LEFT The Lingyansi (Magic Cliff) Temple. China. Werner Forman/WERNER FORMAN/arcaid.co.uk.

22 TOP RIGHT Provence, France. Richard Bryant/arcaid.co.uk.

22 BOTTOM LEFT Prague, Czech Republic. Richard Bryant/arcaid.co.uk.

22 BOTTOM RIGHT Chefchaouen, Morocco. Natalie Tepper/arcaid.co.uk.

23 TOP Portable altars are often kept in the upper room accessible through the shuttered passage above the door. Werner Forman/WERNER FORMAN/arcaid.co.uk.

23 BOTTOM The incised entrance stone in front of the mouth of the passage to the burial chamber at Newgrange, Ireland. Werner Forman/WERNER FORMAN/arcaid.co.uk.

24 Matmata, Tunisia. Rainer Kiedrowski/Bildarchiv-Monheim/arcaid.co.uk.

25 LEFT The Cliff Palace. Mesa Verde, Colorado, United States. Werner Forman/WERNER FORMAN/arcaid.co.uk.

25 RIGHT Trulli stone dwelling. Alberobello, Italy. Valeria Carullo/arcaid.co.uk.

26 TOP LEFT Sidi Bou Said, Tunisia. Natalie Tepper/arcaid.co.uk.

26 TOP RIGHT Traditional Berber village. Tamezret, Tunisia. Natalie Tepper/arcaid.co.uk.

26 BOTTOM Nissiros, Monastery Trini. Dodecanese, Greece. Rainer Kiedrowski/Bildarchiv-Monheim/arcaid.co.uk.

27 TOP Santorini, Greece. Rainer Kiedrowski/Bildarchiv-Monheim/arcaid.co.uk.

27 BOTTOM Santorini, Greece. Rainer Kiedrowski/Bildarchiv-Monheim/arcaid.co.uk.

28 TOP Chefchaouen, Morocco. Natalie Tepper/arcaid.co.uk.

28 BOTTOM LEFT Chefchaouen, Morocco. Natalie Tepper/arcaid.co.uk.

28 BOTTOM RIGHT Chefchaouen, Morocco. Natalie Tepper/arcaid.co.uk.

29 TOP Chefchaouen, Morocco. Natalie Tepper/arcaid.co.uk.

29 BOTTOM Entrance to the home and museum of sculptor Antonio Canova. Possagno, Italy. Richard Bryant/arcaid.co.uk.

30 TOP Venice, Italy. Mike Burton/arcaid.co.uk.

30 BOTTOM LEFT Chelsea, London. Richard Bryant/arcaid.co.uk.

30 BOTTOM RIGHT Chimney Pot Park. Manchester, England, UK. arcaid.co.uk.

31 TOP Chefchaouen, Morocco. Natalie Tepper/arcaid.co.uk.

31 BOTTOM LEFT Blue painted stable split door with leaded window in white painted house with iron railings. David Mark Soulsby/arcaid.co.uk.

31 BOTTOM RIGHT Halifax, Nova Scotia, Canada. Natalie Tepper/arcaid.co.uk.

32 TOP LEFT La Mezquita. Cordoba, Spain. Colin Dixon/arcaid.co.uk.

32 TOP RIGHT Jaffa, Israel. Robert O'Dea/arcaid.co.uk.

32 BOTTOM LEFT Riyadh, Saudi Arabia. Robert O'Dea/arcaid.co.uk.

32 BOTTOM RIGHT Procida, Italy. Robert O'Dea/arcaid.co.uk.

33 TOP La Mezquita. Cordoba, Spain. Colin Dixon/arcaid.co.uk.

33 BOTTOM The 12th century tympanum at Saint-Foy abbey church. Conques, France. Jordan Worek.

34 TOP LEFT Sculptural relief above a doorway. La Martyre, Brittany, France. Joe Cornish/arcaid.co.uk.

34 TOP RIGHT An elaborate stone entranceway leading to a fashionable restaurant. Dubrovnik, Croatia. Jordan Worek.

34 BOTTOM LEFT Norman Arched Doorway with 'dog-Toothing' Pattern. Cumbria, England, UK. Colin Dixon/arcaid.co.uk.

34 BOTTOM RIGHT A restored portal with intricate studded woodwork. Prague, Czech Republic. Jordan Worek.

35 TOP Venice, Italy. Annet van der Voort/Bildarchiv-Monheim/arcaid.co.uk.

35 BOTTOM Poblet, Abbey Church Santa Maria. Catalonia, Spain. Schutze+Rodemann/Bildarchiv-Monheim/arcaid.co.uk.

36 Palazzo Abatellis, Regional Gallery of Sicily. Palermo, Italy. Richard Bryant/arcaid.co.uk.

37 Paris, France. Joe Cornish/arcaid.co.uk.

38 TOP LEFT Detail of Ghiberti's Doors at the Duomo. Florence, Italy. David Clapp/arcaid.co.uk.

38 TOP RIGHT Ljubljana, Slovenia. Marcel Malherbe/arcaid.co.uk.

38 BOTTOM LEFT Porch and relief detail. Hampstead, London, England, UK. Richard Bryant/arcaid.co.uk.

38 BOTTOM RIGHT Chichester Cathedral. Sussex, England, UK. Mark Fiennes/arcaid.co.uk.

39 TOP Veneto, Italy. Joe Cornish/arcaid.co.uk.

39 BOTTOM Bronze door of Duomo. Campania, Italy. Joe Cornish/arcaid.co.uk.

40 Istanbul, Turkey. Richard Bryant/arcaid.co.uk.

41 TOP LEFT Huesca Cathedral. Aragon, Spain. Markus Bassler/Bildarchiv-Monheim/arcaid.co.uk.

41 TOP RIGHT Baroque doorway. Puglia, Italy. Valeria Carullo/arcaid.co.uk.

41 BOTTOM LEFT Salzburg, Austria. Barbara Opitz/Bildarchiv-Monheim/arcaid.co.uk.

41 BOTTOM RIGHT Nimes, Diana Temple. Provence, France. Achim Bednorz/Bildarchiv-Monheim/arcaid.co.uk.

PHOTO CREDITS

42 TOP LEFT Klostergebäude, Germany. Peter Eberts/Bildarchiv-Monheim/arcaid.co.uk.

42 TOP RIGHT Hühnermarkt, Germany. Florian Monheim/Bildarchiv-Monheim/arcaid.co.uk.

42 BOTTOM LEFT A door and knocker from a home in Venice, Italy, Jordan Worek.

42 BOTTOM RIGHT Carved door panels from the Church of Saints Come and Damien, built about 1530, in St. Come d'Olt, France. Jordan Worek.

43 Provence, France. Achim Bednorz/Bildarchiv-Monheim/arcaid.co.uk.

44 Munich, Germany. Jan-Frederik Waeller/Fabpics/arcaid.co.uk.

45 TOP Dresden, Germany. Florian Monheim/Bildarchiv-Monheim/arcaid.co.uk.

45 BOTTOM The ornate portal with stone figures of a fashionable home in Paris, France. Jordan Worek.

46 TOP LEFT Aljaferya Palace. Zaragoza, Spain. G Jackson/Arcaid/arcaid.co.uk.

46 BOTTOM LEFT The mosque of Sidi Boumédienne. Tlemcen, Algeria. Werner Forman/WERNER FORMAN/arcaid.co.uk.

46 RIGHT Prague, Czech Republic. Richard Bryant/arcaid.co.uk.

47 Cap d'Antibes, France. Richard Bryant/arcaid.co.uk.

48 LEFT Granada, Spain. Herbert Monheim/Bildarchiv-Monheim/arcaid.co.uk.

48 RIGHT Granada, Spain. Herbert Monheim/Bildarchiv-Monheim/arcaid.co.uk.

49 Granada, Spain. Herbert Monheim/Bildarchiv-Monheim/arcaid.co.uk.

50 City Palace. Rajasthan, India. Richard Bryant/arcaid.co.uk.

51 TOP Palazzo Davanzati. Florence, Italy. Richard Bryant/arcaid.co.uk.

51 BOTTOM LEFT Cairo, Egypt. David Clapp/arcaid.co.uk.

51 BOTTOM RIGHT Cairo, Egypt. David Clapp/arcaid.co.uk.

52 TOP LEFT The Alhambra. Granada, Spain. Werner Forman/WERNER FORMAN/arcaid.co.uk.

52 TOP RIGHT Marrakech, Morocco. Natalie Tepper/arcaid.co.uk.

52 BOTTOM LEFT Al-Rifa'i Mosque. Cairo, Egypt. David Clapp/arcaid.co.uk.

52 BOTTOM RIGHT Court of the Maidens at the Alcazar. Seville, Spain. Werner Forman/WERNER FORMAN/arcaid.co.uk.

53 TOP Red Fort (Lal Qila). Delhi, India. Archenova/arcaid.co.uk.

53 BOTTOM Red Fort (Lal Qila). Delhi, India. Archenova/arcaid.co.uk.

54 Nineteenth century richly carved and gilded doors. Bali, Indonesia. Werner Forman/WERNER FORMAN/arcaid.co.uk.

55 Elaborately carved double doors in the Court of the Maidens at the Alcazar. Seville, Spain. Werner Forman/WERNER FORMAN/arcaid.co.uk.

56 TOP Dar Chraiet Museum. Tozeur, Tunisia. Natalie Tepper/arcaid.co.uk.

56 BOTTOM LEFT Palazzo Davanzati. Florence, Italy. Richard Bryant/arcaid.co.uk.

56 BOTTOM RIGHT Marrakech, Morocco. Natalie Tepper/arcaid.co.uk.

57 The Alcazar. Seville, Spain. Werner Forman/WERNER FORMAN/arcaid.co.uk.

58 TOP LEFT City Palace. Rajasthan, India. Richard Bryant/arcaid.co.uk.

58 TOP RIGHT Palazzo Abatellis, Regional Gallery of Sicily. Palermo, Italy. Richard Bryant/arcaid.co.uk.

58 BOTTOM LEFT Casa de Pilatos. Seville, Spain. Richard Bryant/arcaid.co.uk.

58 BOTTOM RIGHT Palazzo Abatellis, Regional Gallery of Sicily. Palermo, Italy. Richard Bryant/arcaid.co.uk.

59 Casa de Pilatos. Seville, Spain. Richard Bryant/arcaid.co.uk.

60 TOP LEFT Florence, Italy. Mike Burton/arcaid.co.uk.

60 TOP RIGHT Venice, Italy. Mike Burton/arcaid.co.uk.

60 BOTTOM LEFT Casa de Pilatos. Seville, Spain. Robert O'Dea/arcaid.co.uk.

60 BOTTOM RIGHT Khiva, Uzbekistan. Flore Lamoureux/arcaid.co.uk.

61 TOP Red Fort (Lal Qila), Delhi, India. Archenova/arcaid.co.uk.

61 BOTTOM Red Fort (Lal Qila), Delhi, India. Archenova/arcaid.co.uk.

62 TOP LEFT Bexleyheath, London, England, UK. Charlotte Wood/arcaid.co.uk.

62 TOP RIGHT Chefchaouen, Morocco. Natalie Tepper/arcaid.co.uk.

62 BOTTOM LEFT Venice, Italy. Mike Burton/arcaid.co.uk.

62 BOTTOM RIGHT Venice, Italy. Mike Burton/arcaid.co.uk.

63 TOP LEFT Bahia Palace. Marrakech, Morocco. Natalie Tepper/arcaid.co.uk.

63 TOP RIGHT Red Fort (Lal Qila), Delhi, India. Archenova/arcaid.co.uk.

63 BOTTOM Red Fort (Lal Qila), Delhi, India. Archenova/arcaid.co.uk.

63 TOP LEFT Florence, Italy. Mike Burton/arcaid.co.uk.

64 TOP RIGHT Florence, Italy. Mike Burton/arcaid.co.uk.

64 BOTTOM Delhi, India. Archenova/arcaid.co.uk.

65 TOP Bruchsal, Germany. Florian Monheim/Bildarchiv-Monheim/arcaid.co.uk.

65 BOTTOM LEFT Venice, Italy. Mike Burton/arcaid.co.uk.

65 BOTTOM RIGHT Florence, Italy. Mike Burton/arcaid.co.uk.

66 Burgundy, France. Paul M.R. Maeyaert/Bildarchiv-Monheim/arcaid.co.uk.

67 The Lutfullah Mosque. Isfahan, Iran. Will Pryce/Thames & Hudson/arcaid.co.uk.

68 LEFT Sidi Bou Said, Tunisia. Natalie Tepper/arcaid.co.uk.

68 RIGHT Chefchaouen, Morocco. Natalie Tepper/arcaid.co.uk.

69 LEFT Chefchaouen, Morocco. Natalie Tepper/arcaid.co.uk.

69 RIGHT Chefchaouen, Morocco. Natalie Tepper/arcaid.co.uk.

70 TOP LEFT Court of the Maidens at the Alcazar. Seville, Spain. Werner Forman/WERNER FORMAN/arcaid.co.uk.

70 BOTTOM Al-Suhaymi House. Cairo, Egypt. David Clapp/arcaid.co.uk.

71 TOP Rabat, Morocco. Natalie Tepper/arcaid.co.uk.

71 BOTTOM LEFT The mosque of Sidi Boumédienne. Tlemcen, Algeria. Door. Werner Forman/WERNER FORMAN/arcaid.co.uk.

71 BOTTOM RIGHT Court of the Maidens at the Alcazar. Seville, Spain. Werner Forman/WERNER FORMAN/arcaid.co.uk.

72 TOP LEFT Brass Spider door knob. David Churchill/arcaid.co.uk.

72 TOP RIGHT Rotherwick Church. Hampshire, England, UK. Olwen Croft/arcaid.co.uk.

72 BOTTOM LEFT Cornwall, England, UK. Ruth Marler/arcaid.co.uk.

72 BOTTOM RIGHT Il de Re, France. Olwen Croft/arcaid.co.uk.

73 Ramble, France. Lucinda Lambton/arcaid.co.uk.

74 TOP City Palace. Rajasthan, India. Richard Bryant/arcaid.co.uk.

74 BOTTOM Rio de Janeiro, Brazil. Alan Weintraub/arcaid.co.uk.

75 TOP Naples, Italy. Richard Bryant/arcaid.co.uk.

75 BOTTOM Lower Saxony, Alfeld, Germany. Gillian Darley/Edifice/arcaid.co.uk.

PHOTO CREDITS

180 TOP RIGHT Antwerp, Belgium. Paul M.R. Maeyaert/Bildarchiv-Monheim/arcaid.co.uk.

180 BOTTOM LEFT Catalonia, Spain. Schutze+Rodemann/Bildarchiv-Monheim/arcaid.co.uk.

180 BOTTOM RIGHT The Renaissance "House at the Two Golden Bears" in Prague, Czech Republic, is famous for its ornate portal with bear reliefs. Jordan Worek

181 A late gothic door leading to the Old Town Hall in Prague, Czech Republic. Jordan Worek.

182 TOP LEFT Rhodes Old Town, Greece. David Churchill/arcaid.co.uk.

182 TOP RIGHT Veneto, Italy. Fabio Zoratti/arcaid.co.uk.

182 BOTTOM LEFT Hambacher, Germany. Florian Monheim/Bildarchiv-Monheim/arcaid.co.uk.

182 BOTTOM RIGHT Le Puy Cathedral. Haute-Loire, France. Paul M.R. Maeyaert/Bildarchiv-Monheim/arcaid.co.uk.

183 TOP LEFT Indre, France. Paul M.R. Maeyaert/Bildarchiv-Monheim/arcaid.co.uk.

183 TOP RIGHT Hambacher Schloss, Germany. Florian Monheim/Bildarchiv-Monheim/arcaid.co.uk.

183 BOTTOM LEFT Milan, Italy. G Jackson/Arcaid/arcaid.co.uk.

183 BOTTOM RIGHT Tuscany, Italy. Herbert Monheim/Bildarchiv-Monheim/arcaid.co.uk.

184 TOP LEFT Vila Real, Portugal. Markus Bassler/Bildarchiv-Monheim/arcaid.co.uk.

184 TOP RIGHT Veneto, Italy. Fabio Zoratti/arcaid.co.uk.

184 BOTTOM LEFT Veneto, Italy. Fabio Zoratti/arcaid.co.uk.

184 BOTTOM RIGHT Cornwall, England, UK. Philippa Lewis/Edifice/arcaid.co.uk.

185 TOP LEFT Saale, Germany. Schutze+Rodemann/Bildarchiv-Monheim/arcaid.co.uk.

185 TOP RIGHT Veneto, Italy. Fabio Zoratti/arcaid.co.uk.

185 BOTTOM LEFT Granada, Spain. Achim Bednorz/Bildarchiv-Monheim/arcaid.co.uk.

185 BOTTOM RIGHT Andalusia, Spain. Markus Bassler/Bildarchiv-Monheim/arcaid.co.uk.

186 TOP Walworth, London, England, UK. Richard Bryant/arcaid.co.uk.

186 BOTTOM George Blossom House, 4858 Kenwood Avenue. Chicago, Illinois, United States. Alan Weintraub/arcaid.co.uk.

187 No 9 Millbank, London, England, UK. Richard Bryant/arcaid.co.uk.

188 TOP LEFT Baroque Palazzo. Rome, Italy. Robert O'Dea/arcaid.co.uk.

188 TOP RiGHT Hradcany District. Prague, Czech Republic. Olwen Croft/arcaid.co.uk.

188 BOTTOM LEFT Mala Strana District. Prague, Czech Republic. Natalie Tepper/arcaid.co.uk.

188 BOTTOM RIGHT Ivy growing on wall above studded carved wood double doors. Karl-Dietrich Buhler/EWA/arcaid.co.uk.

189 Burgos Cathedral. Old Castile, Spain. Markus Bassler/Bildarchiv-Monheim/arcaid.co.uk.

190 Blackwell house restoration, Lake District. View of hall from dining room. Charlotte Wood/arcaid.co.uk.

191 TOP LEFT Elephant's Head Door Knockers. Warwick Lane, London, England, UK. Richard Turpin/arcaid.co.uk.

191 TOP RIGHT Bamberg, Germany. Peter Eberts/Bildarchiv-Monheim/arcaid.co.uk.

191 BOTTOM LEFT Horse Head Door Handle, University Library, Ljublijana, Slovenia. Mark Fiennes/arcaid.co.uk.

191 BOTTOM RIGHT Handle on the door to the sacristy Sacred Heart Church. Prague, Czech Republic. Mark Fiennes/arcaid.co.uk.

192-193 TOP London, England, UK. Richard Bryant/arcaid.co.uk.

192 BOTTOM LEFT Chelsea, London, England, UK. Tim Mitchell/arcaid.co.uk.

192 BOTTOM RIGHT London, England, UK. Richard Bryant/arcaid.co.uk.

193 BOTTOM LEFT New brick house with white front door and canopy. Benedict Luxmoore/arcaid.co.uk.

193 BOTTOM RIGHT Mark Fiennes/arcaid.co.uk.

194 TOP LEFT Chelsea, London, England, UK. Tim Mitchell/arcaid.co.uk.

194 TOP RIGHT Chelsea, London, England, UK. Tim Mitchell/arcaid.co.uk.

194 BOTTOM LEFT 10 Downing Street. London, England, UK. Mark Fiennes/arcaid.co.uk.

194 BOTTOM RIGHT Sussex, England, UK. Lucinda Lambton/arcaid.co.uk.

195 Derbyshire, England, UK. Richard Bryant/arcaid.co.uk.

196 TOP LEFT Georgian double-fronted house with pedimented portico supported by ionic columns approached by flagstone path bordered by lavender. David Mark Soulsby/arcaid.co.uk.

196 TOP RIGHT White front door on white Victorian house. David Markson/EWA/arcaid.co.uk.

196 BOTTOM LEFT Wide wood paneled door in red brick house approached by white painted steps and tessellated terracotta tiles with planted pots on steps. David Mark Soulsby/arcaid.co.uk.

196 BOTTOM RIGHT Kensington, London, England, UK. Robert O'Dea/arcaid.co.uk.

197 TOP LEFT Close-up of front door of traditional Victorian house. Dominic Whiting/EWA/arcaid.co.uk.

197 TOP RIGHT Close-up of stained glass panels in black Victorian front door. David Markson/EWA/arcaid.co.uk.

197 BOTTOM LEFT Corner entrance door to traditional apartment block flanked by black urns on pedestals containing topiary. David Mark Soulsby/arcaid.co.uk.

197 BOTTOM RIGHT Chelsea, London, England, UK. Tim Mitchell/arcaid.co.uk.

198 TOP LEFT St Christopher's Church. Lancashire, England, UK. Mark Fiennes/arcaid.co.uk.

198 TOP MIDDLE Door knocker. Mark Fiennes/arcaid.co.uk.

198 TOP RIGHT Devon, England, UK. Richard Bryant/arcaid.co.uk.

198 MIDDLE LEFT Prague, Czech Republic. Olwen Croft/arcaid.co.uk.

198 MIDDLE CENTER Prague, Czech Republic. Mark Fiennes/arcaid.co.uk.

198 MIDDLE RIGHT Debenham House. London, England, UK. Lucinda Lambton/arcaid.co.uk.

198 BOTTOM LEFT 10 Downing Street. London, England, UK. Mark Fiennes/arcaid.co.uk.

198 BOTTOM MIDDLE Brussels, Belgium. Richard Bryant/arcaid.co.uk.

198 BOTTOM RIGHT Little Thakeham. Sussex, England, UK. Lucinda Lambton/arcaid.co.uk.

199 West Midlands, UK. Richard Bryant/arcaid.co.uk.

200 Royal Academy of Arts, Burlington House. London, England, UK. Richard Bryant/arcaid.co.uk.

201 Home of George Washington. Mount Vernon, Virginia, United States. Richard Bryant/arcaid.co.uk.

202 Treviso, Italy. Richard Bryant/arcaid.co.uk.

203 TOP Door detail with gilded pediment and pilaster. London, England, UK. Richard Bryant/arcaid.co.uk.

203 BOTTOM Piccadilly, London, England, UK. Richard Bryant/arcaid.co.uk.

204 TOP LEFT Close up of metal door knocker. Premium/arcaid.co.uk.

204 Detail of ornate door with key shaped handle. Amsterdam, The Netherlands. Alex Bartel/arcaid.co.uk.

204 MIDDLE LEFT Door with 19th century brass keyhole covers. Nottinghamshire, England, UK. Lucinda Lambton/arcaid.co.uk.

204 MIDDLE CENTER Isle of Bute, Scotland. Lucinda Lambton/arcaid.co.uk.

204 MIDDLE RIGHT Berkshire, England, UK. Lucinda Lambton/arcaid.co.uk.

204 BOTTOM LEFT Isle of Bute, Scotland. Lucinda Lambton/arcaid.co.uk.

204 BOTTOM RIGHT Glin Castle, Ireland. Joe Cornish/arcaid.co.uk.

206 TOP Antiquarian Bookshop. Prague, Czech Republic. Natalie Tepper/arcaid.co.uk.

206 BOTTOM LEFT San Gimignano, Italy. Mike Burton/arcaid.co.uk.

206 BOTTOM RIGHT Venice, Italy. Mike Burton/arcaid.co.uk.

207 Venice, Italy. Natalie Tepper/arcaid.co.uk.

208 TOP LEFT Venice, Italy. Mike Burton/arcaid.co.uk.

208 TOP RIGHT Period Old Dairy Shop, Columbia Market. London, England, UK. Mark Bury/arcaid.co.uk.

208 BOTTOM LEFT Venice, Italy. Mike Burton/arcaid.co.uk.

208 BOTTOM RIGHT Venice, Italy. Mike Burton/arcaid.co.uk.

209 TOP LEFT Venice, Italy. Mike Burton/arcaid.co.uk.

209 TOP RIGHT San Gimignano, Italy. Mike Burton/arcaid.co.uk.

209 BOTTOM LEFT Venice, Italy. Mike Burton/arcaid.co.uk.

209 BOTTOM RIGHT San Gimignano, Italy. Mike Burton/arcaid.co.uk.

210 TOP Waverley, Columbus, Mississippi, United States. Richard Bryant/arcaid.co.uk.

210 BOTTOM LEFT Salem, Massachusetts, United States. Richard Bryant/Gardner-Pingree House/arcaid.co.uk.

210 BOTTOM RIGHT Potsdam, Germany. Richard Bryant/arcaid.co.uk.

211 Royal Palace, Madrid, Spain. Richard Bryant/arcaid.co.uk.

212 Treviso, Italy. Richard Bryant/arcaid.co.uk.

213 Derbyshire, England. Richard Bryant/arcaid.co.uk.

214 TOP Hancock Shaker Village, Massachusetts, United States. Richard Bryant/arcaid.co.uk.

214 BOTTOM LEFT Toro Canyon House. Monecito, California, United States. Richard Powers/arcaid.co.uk.

214 BOTTOM RIGHT Ito, Japan. Ian Lambot/arcaid.co.uk.

215 TOP Belgravia, London, England, UK. Richard Bryant/arcaid.co.uk

215 BOTTOM LEFT Inglaterra House, Brazil. Alan Weintraub/arcaid.co.uk.

215 BOTTOM RIGHT Auckland, New Zealand. Richard Powers/arcaid.co.uk.

216 TOP Casa Pau Ferro, Brazil. Alan Weintraub/arcaid.co.uk.

216 BOTTOM Dublin, Ireland. arcaid.co.uk.

217 TOP São Paulo, Brazil. Alan Weintraub/arcaid.co.uk.

217 BOTTOM The William Herman Winslow House. River Forest, Illinois, United States. Alan Weintraub/arcaid.co.uk.

218 LEFT Musterhäuser, Germany. Florian Monheim/Bildarchiv-Monheim/arcaid.co.uk.

218 RIGHT Alfeld, Germany. Achim Bednorz/Bildarchiv-Monheim/arcaid.co.uk.

219 George C Stockman House, Mason City, Iowa, United States. Alan Weintraub/arcaid.co.uk.

220 TOP The Hollyhock House / Aline Barnsdall House. Los Angeles, California, United States. Thomas A. Heinz/arcaid.co.uk.

220 BOTTOM The William B. Tracy House. Normandy Park, Washington, United States. Alan Weintraub/arcaid.co.uk.

221 TOP Susan Lawrence Dana House / Dana-Thomas House. Springfield, Illinois, United States. Alan Weintraub/arcaid.co.uk.

221 BOTTOM The Arthur Heurtley House. Oak Park, Illinois, United States. Alan Weintraub/arcaid.co.uk.

222 LEFT Chateau de Saumur. Val de Loire, France. Florian Monheim/Bildarchiv-Monheim/arcaid.co.uk.

222 RIGHT Carcassonne, France. Mark Fiennes/arcaid.co.uk.

223 TOP Brasilia Theater, Brazil. Alan Weintraub/arcaid.co.uk.

223 BOTTOM Brasilia, Memorial dos Povos Indigenes. Brazil. Alan Weintraub/arcaid.co.uk.

224 TOP Isfahan, Iran. Will Pryce/Thames & Hudson/arcaid.co.uk.

224 BOTTOM Bukhara, Uzbekistan. Will Pryce/Thames & Hudson/arcaid.co.uk.

225 TOP Veneto, Italy. G. Paolo Marton/Bildarchiv-Monheim/arcaid.co.uk.

225 BOTTOM LEFT Hearst Tower. New York, New York, United States. Chuck Choi/arcaid.co.uk.

225 BOTTOM RIGHT Surbiton Railway Station. Surrey, England, UK. G Jackson/Arcaid/arcaid.co.uk.

226 Brion Cemetery. Treviso, Italy. Richard Bryant/arcaid.co.uk.

227 TOP LEFT Hampstead, London, England, UK. Nicholas Kane/arcaid.co.uk.

227 TOP RIGHT São Paolo, Brazil. Alan Weintraub/arcaid.co.uk.

227 BOTTOM Sheats Goldstein House. Los Angeles, California, United States. Alan Weintraub/arcaid.co.uk.

228 LEFT Chelsea, London, England, UK. Tim Mitchell/arcaid.co.uk.

228 RIGHT London, England, UK. Richard Bryant/arcaid.co.uk.

229 LEFT São Paulo, Brazil. Alan Weintraub/arcaid.co.uk.

229 RIGHT Garden Studio. Wiltshire, England, UK. Ben Luxmoore/arcaid.co.uk.

230 TOP LEFT Camden Town, London, England, UK. Richard Bryant/arcaid.co.uk.

230 TOP RIGHT São Paulo, Brazil. Alan Weintraub/arcaid.co.uk.

230 BOTTOM Camden Town, London, England, UK. Richard Bryant/arcaid.co.uk.

231 TOP LEFT Ad Astra. Rear double height doors. Richard Bryant/arcaid.co.uk.

231 TOP RIGHT Brazil. Alan Weintraub/arcaid.co.uk.

231 BOTTOM Casa Darmos. Tivissa, Spain. Eugeni Pons/arcaid.co.uk.

232 TOP LEFT Plettenberg Bay, South Africa. Richard Bryant/arcaid.co.uk.

232 TOP RIGHT Beyer House. Malibu, California, United States. Alan Weintraub/arcaid.co.uk.

232 BOTTOM Carlos Bratke House. São Paulo, Brazil. Alan Weintraub/arcaid.co.uk.

PHOTO INDEX